THE BOY WHO LOVED BIRDS

This book belongs to

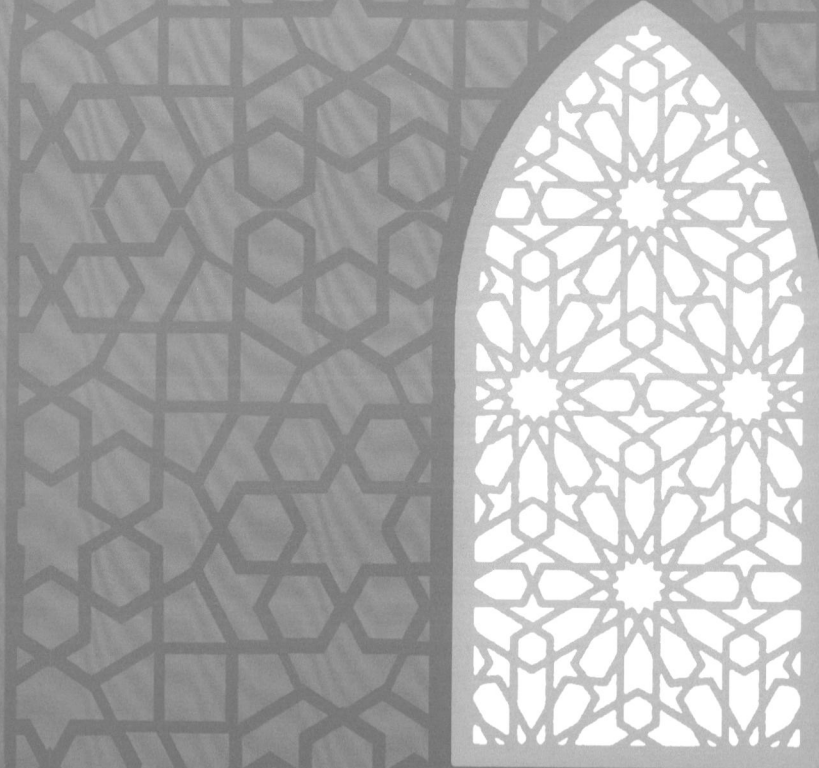

**Read more in the Dreamers series by
Lavanya Karthik**

dreamers

THE BOY WHO LOVED BIRDS

SALIM ALI

Written and illustrated by

LAVANYA KARTHIK

duckbill

An imprint of Penguin Random House

For you, and the curious music your heart follows.

DUCKBILL BOOKS

USA | Canada | UK | Ireland | Australia
New Zealand | India | South Africa | China | Singapore

Duckbill Books is part of the Penguin Random House group of companies
whose addresses can be found at global.penguinrandomhouse.com

Published by Penguin Random House India Pvt. Ltd
4th Floor, Capital Tower 1, MG Road,
Gurugram 122 002, Haryana, India

First published in Duckbill Books by
Penguin Random House India 2022

Text and illustrations copyright © Lavanya Karthik 2022

10 9 8 7 6 5 4

This book is, as the author claims, a work of 'faction' and, while fixed both historically
and chronologically, remains fiction, based on fact, embroidered and distorted in order
to project the character herein. All names, save where obviously genuine, are fictitious
and any resemblance to persons living or dead is wholly coincidental.

ISBN 9780143457732

Typeset in Georgia by DiTech Publishing Services Pvt. Ltd
Printed at Paras Offset Pvt. Ltd., Kundli (Haryana)

www.penguin.co.in

DR SALIM ALI

Dr Salim Ali is often called the Birdman of India. He laid the foundations of ornithology (the study of birds) in the country.

But before he became the Birdman of India, he was a boy called Saloo, with an airgun in one hand and a mystery in the other.

This is his story.

What is a bird?

A target for sport.

A morsel to savour.

A pet.

A bird is a simple thing,
thinks Saloo.

Until he meets a **mystery**.

What is the mystery?

A bird Saloo has never seen before.

A puzzle he wants to solve.

The start of a great journey.

Across town, says Uncle Amir, lies the answer to his puzzle. But is Saloo brave enough to find it?

Saloo's heart soars, then falls. For the Empire that holds his land in its cruel grip cares little for curious Indian boys.

Dare he take his questions to its door?

वन्देमातरं

But the mystery hums its curious tune, and the beat of his heart must follow.

Across town he journeys in search
of his answer . . .

until he stands before a stately doorway, and faces a stern doorman.

The mystery gleams with its
curious light, that his heart and feet
must follow.

Up a great stairway,

past walls lined with
terrifying trophies,

down long corridors,
towards the answer
he seeks.

Who will he meet?

What will he find?

Fear freezes his feet!

Until the
mystery flutters
its curious wings.

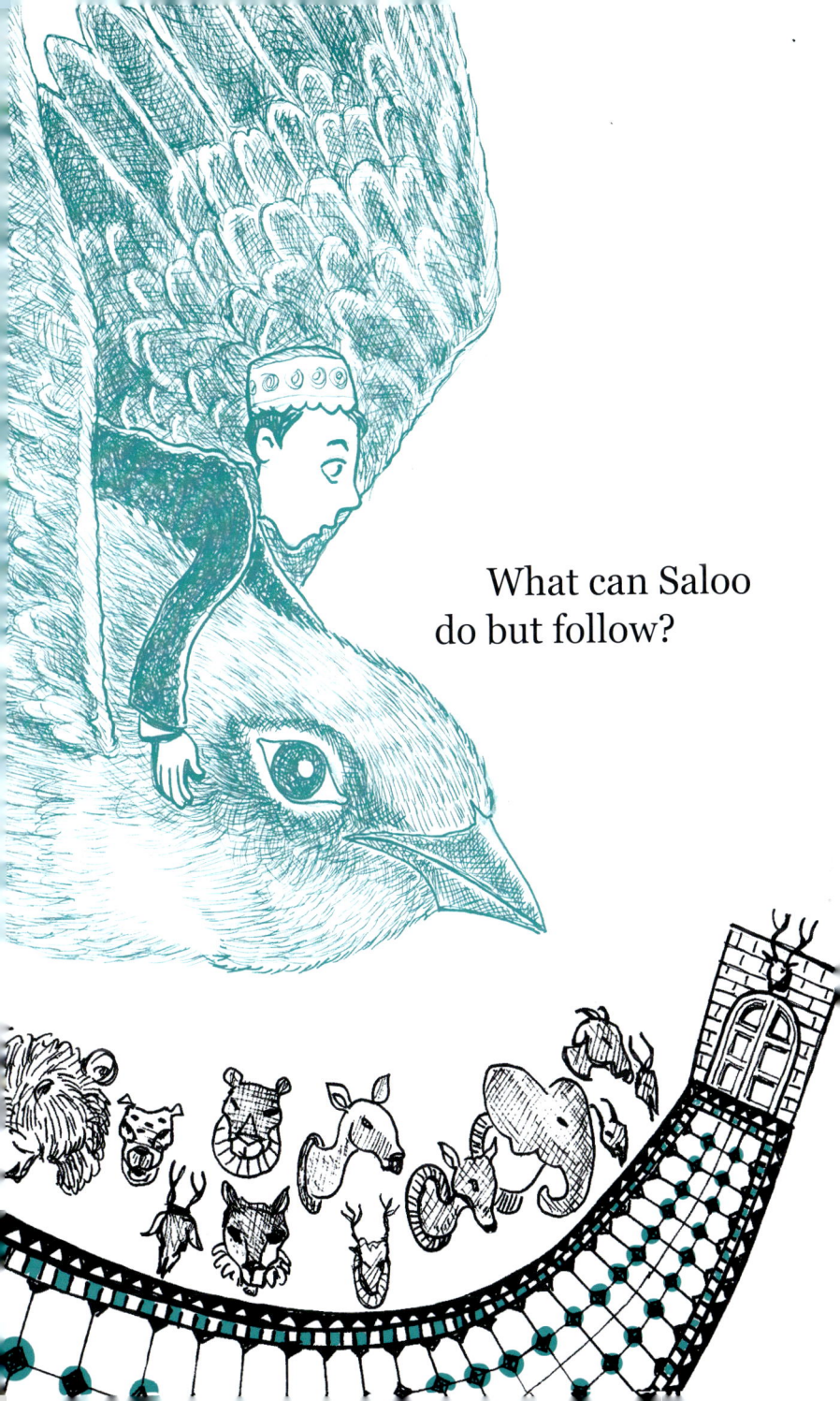

What can Saloo
do but follow?

'Come in!' says the man waiting within.

And he delights at the sight of the mystery.

W.S. MILLARD

'It's a yellow-throated sparrow!' the man says.

'But sparrows are always just white and brown!' Saloo says. 'Aren't they?'

The man's smile widens. 'Come! See for yourself!'

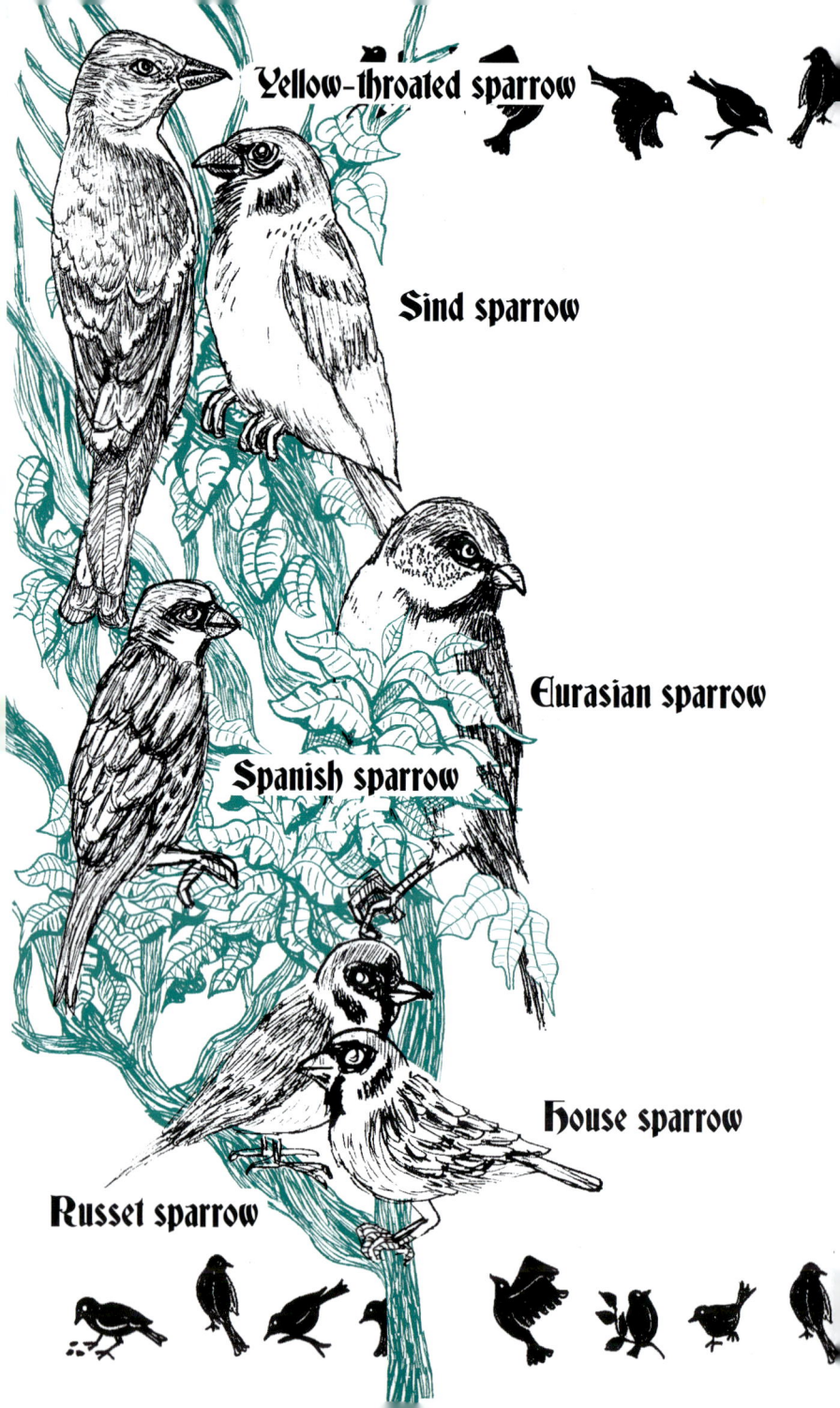

Yellow-throated sparrow

Sind sparrow

Eurasian sparrow

Spanish sparrow

House sparrow

Russet sparrow

What does Saloo see?

A museum of birds, carefully collected and preserved.

A room filled with mysteries like his own, solved with love and care.

A treasure for curious minds and hearts, that care little for the ways of Empires.

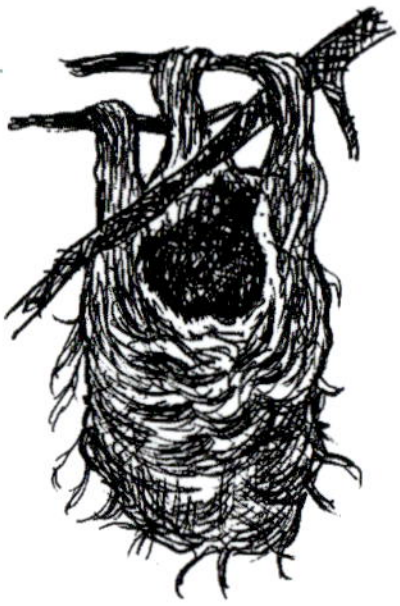

What is a bird?

No longer a simple thing.
A **marvel** of science.
A creature of **variety**.
A **world of mystery** still
waiting to be explored.

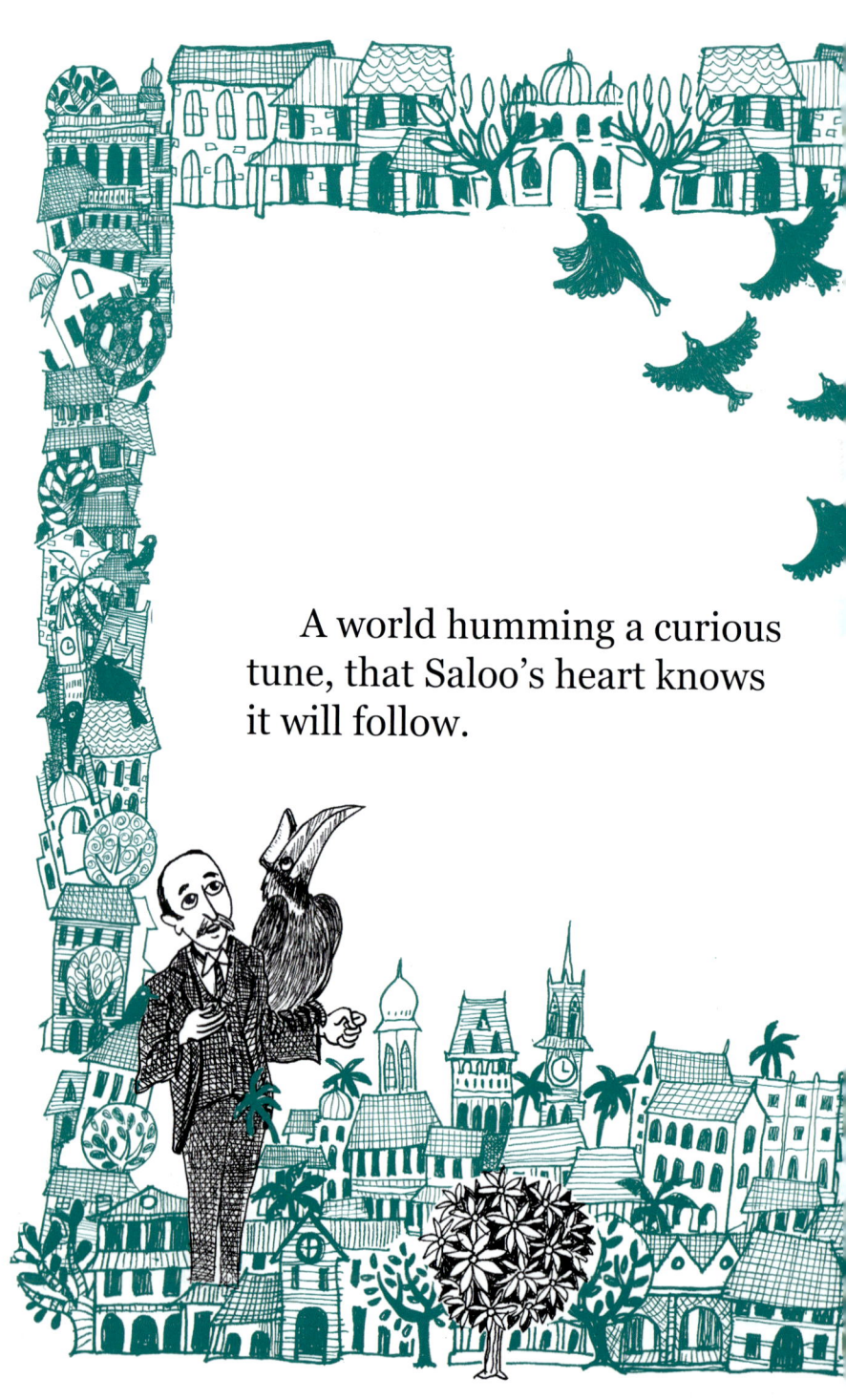

A world humming a curious tune, that Saloo's heart knows it will follow.

What is a bird?

Saloo finds his answer in the years that follow—years that he fills with treasures of his own.

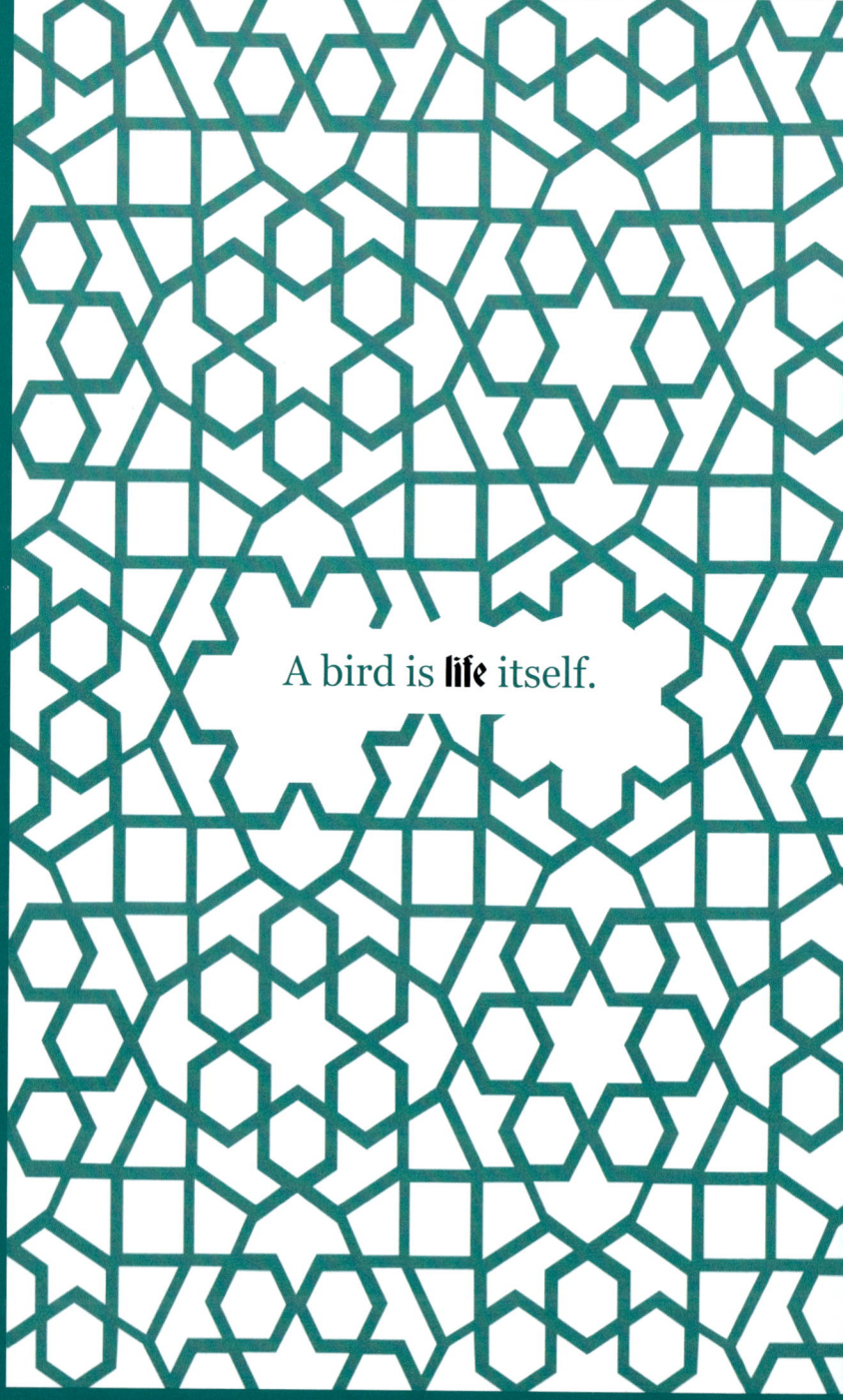

A bird is **life** itself.

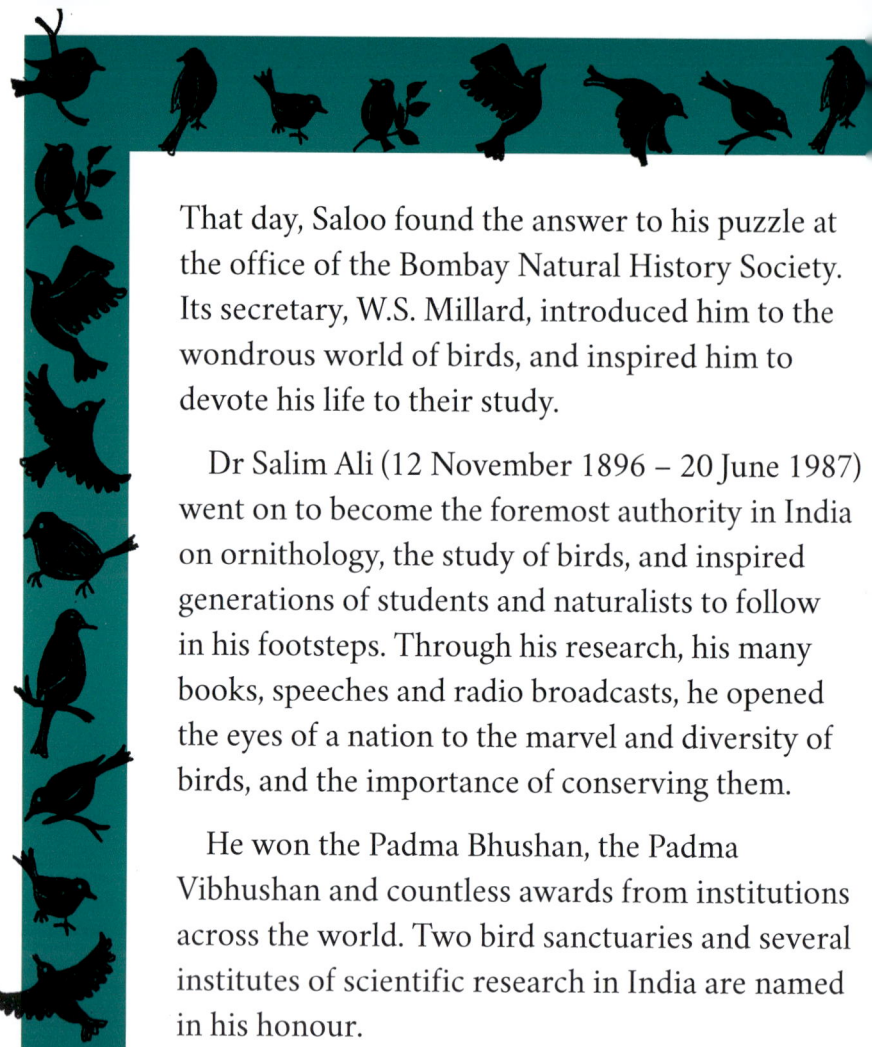

That day, Saloo found the answer to his puzzle at the office of the Bombay Natural History Society. Its secretary, W.S. Millard, introduced him to the wondrous world of birds, and inspired him to devote his life to their study.

Dr Salim Ali (12 November 1896 – 20 June 1987) went on to become the foremost authority in India on ornithology, the study of birds, and inspired generations of students and naturalists to follow in his footsteps. Through his research, his many books, speeches and radio broadcasts, he opened the eyes of a nation to the marvel and diversity of birds, and the importance of conserving them.

He won the Padma Bhushan, the Padma Vibhushan and countless awards from institutions across the world. Two bird sanctuaries and several institutes of scientific research in India are named in his honour.

The illustrations in this book are inspired by miniature art from the Mughal era. Dr Ali loved this art form, especially the paintings of animals and birds.

Meet some of the birds in this book:

The yellow-throated sparrow or
the chestnut-shouldered petronia
(Gymnoris xanthocollis),
which inspired Salim's
interest in birds.

The Himalayan forest
thrush *(Zoothera salimalii),*
one of several species of
birds named after Dr Ali.

William, a great pied hornbill
(Buceros bicornis), who lived for
over two decades in the office of the
BNHS. The current premises of the
Society were named Hornbill House
in his memory.

The author wishes to thank
Zai Whitaker, Tara Gandhi and the BNHS archives
for their help in the making of this book.

Lavanya Karthik is an author and illustrator by day, a cookie monster by teatime, and fast asleep by nine at night. She lives in Mumbai where she eats a lot of chocolate and takes a lot of naps.